Bookworks

Making Books by Hand

Gwenyth Swain
with Minnesota Center for Book Arts

Illustrations by Jennifer Hagerman / Photographs by Andy King

Carolrhoda Books, Inc./Minneapolis

The author wishes to acknowledge the help, cooperation, and encouragement of the staff of Minnesota Center for Book Arts. Many thanks as well to the children who took part in the making of this book.—G.S.

Bookworks was designed by Steve Foley and typeset by Interface Graphics, Inc. The text was set in New Aster, with headings in Lucida Sans. The John Roberts Company printed the book in five colors on 80-pound Moistrite Matte paper. Binding was done by **Muscle Bound Bindery, Inc.**

Library of Congress Cataloging-in-Publication Data

Swain, Gwenyth, 1961-
   Bookworks : making books by hand / Gwenyth Swain with Minnesota Center for Book Arts ; illustrations by Jennifer Hagerman ; photographs by Andy King.
      p. cm.
   Includes bibliographical references (p.).
   ISBN 0-87614-858-5 (lib. bdg.)
   1. Book design—Juvenile literature. [1. Books. 2. Book design. 3. Handicraft.] I. Hagerman, Jennifer, ill. II. King, Andy, ill. III. Minnesota Center for Book Arts. IV. Title.
Z116.A3S93 1995
745.5—dc20   94-28120

Manufactured in the United States of America
  2 3 4 5 6 – JR – 00 99 98 97 96

Metric Conversion Chart

When you know	Multiply by	To find
length		
inches	2.54	centimeters
feet	.3	meters
capacity		
tablespoons	15.0	milliliters
cups	0.24	liters
gallons	3.8	liters

Contents

I. Why Make Books?

Above and opposite page: *Each year at Minnesota Center for Book Arts in Minneapolis, busloads of schoolkids learn about the shapes books can take—and then learn to make books by hand.*

Unlock your diary and you've found a place to put down your most secret thoughts. Open the pages of a book like *Alice in Wonderland* and you can enter an imaginary world. Page through the yellow pages, and if you look long enough, you'll probably find the number you need.

Books can do many different things for readers. They can be a place to record feelings and thoughts or a way to share ideas. They can also be beautiful and fun, especially when they're made by hand.

When you picture a book in your mind, you might think of a heavy gray volume sitting on a dusty, dark shelf. But think again. A handmade book can be as simple or as complex as the maker wants it to be. It can be as tiny as your thumb or as tall as a refrigerator. It can even be shaped like a pyramid or a circle or a fish.

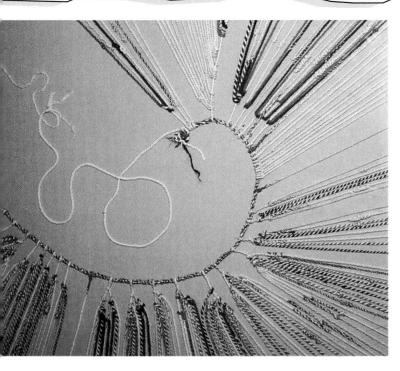

Left: *Although it may look like a bunch of string, this is a kind of accounts book popular in Peru many years ago.*

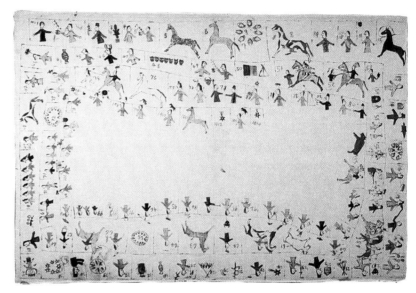

You can tell a story with pictures just as well as with words—something the Dakota Indians of North America understood when they made this book in the 1800s.

In all the thousands of years people have been making them, books have come in all shapes and sizes. Even what people called a book has varied from one culture to another. In Peru, for example, a type of book called a **quipu** (pronounced KEY-pooh) was invented. A quipu was made of many strings tied together. Knots in the strings represented numbers of goods, telling anyone who could read it what the quipu's owner owned.

In Native North America, people wrote on animal skins, wood, bark, and cloth. Native American bookmakers normally used pictures and symbols rather than letters and words to tell their stories.

In Thailand and other parts of Asia, people wanted to be able to add onto their books easily. They made books that look a bit like window blinds. When they had a new idea that just had to go into a book, they simply glued on more long, skinny folded pages.

For as long as people have been making books, some creative book-makers have experimented with odd

The maker of this handwritten book of love songs from medieval France knew that the shape of a book can help tell a story.

shapes, sometimes even using a shape that helps tell readers what the book is about. It shouldn't be too hard to guess what this heart-shaped book from the 1400s in France is about. It's filled with love songs.

Folding books may look unusual, but they're very practical, especially if you know you'll need to add pages later.

In the earliest days of writing—and in the days of the very first books—people made books that looked like lumps of clay. That's not surprising. In ancient Mesopotamia, in an area now called the Persian Gulf, people had lots of clay. They also very much needed books, because they were traders and needed to keep track of their goods.

The ancient Mesopotamians created a system of hard clay tokens representing goods. A person who owned sheep, for example, took a token with a design that meant "one sheep" and pressed it into a soft, flat piece of clay called a **tablet**. Once the clay tablet hardened, the owner had a permanent record, a kind of clay accounts book.

By pressing tokens into soft clay and allowing the clay to harden, someone made this tablet book over 5000 years ago.

In ancient Mesopotamia, each of these clay tokens stood for a different item. The token at the far right means "one sheep."

Be a Mesopotamian Bookmaker

You don't have to go all the way to ancient Mesopotamia for a clay tablet. Try taking a hunk of air-dry clay, sold in art supply and hobby stores, and forming it into a tablet shape.

First cover a work surface with old newspaper. Break off a small hunk of clay and form it into a tablet shape.

Write a story in the clay with a stick or pencil. Or try pressing objects into the clay to create interesting designs.

Dry your tablet according to the package instructions. Then use tempera or acrylic paints to decorate it. (If you use tempera paints, use a spray fixative to keep colors from flaking off.)

The first clay tablets were account books, so you could use your tablet to make a record of all the things you own. Or think of your own ten commandments to give to your younger brother or sister.

Above: *These early bookworms lived in the ancient city of Pompeii. The woman on the left holds a wax tablet in one hand, her metal stylus in the other. Her husband has a rolled papyrus scroll tucked under his chin.*
Right: *A wax tablet codex*

It's flat on the other end, which probably kept it from rolling off many Roman tables.

Once a Roman no longer needed what was written on the tablet, the wax could be heated and then smoothed out with the flat end of the stylus. Before long people found that one wax tablet didn't hold all that they wanted to write. People solved this problem by tying two or more tablets together and calling the new object a **codex**. In some countries, the word *codex* is still used to mean a book.

Tablet books weren't all made of clay. In early Rome, a person who wanted to write took a piece of wood, covered it with a thin layer of wax, and pressed words into the wax with something called a **stylus**. A stylus is pointed on one end, making it a good writing tool.

Papyrus plants (above) *still grow in Egypt. Some are harvested to make sheets of papyrus for scrolls just as they were thousands of years ago.* Right: *Papyrus scrolls*

People in ancient Egypt learned to make books from **papyrus,** a plant that grows along the Nile River. Egyptians pounded the plant fibers flat and pasted strips together in long rolls called **scrolls.** Scrolls were easy to make and took up little space. But they had some drawbacks. Like modern videocassettes, scroll books had to be rewound once the reader was finished.

In Europe during the Middle Ages, most people had never seen papyrus. And though paper had been invented in Asia, Europeans hadn't heard the news. Europeans did have calves, sheep, and goats. They discovered that by specially treating calf-, sheep-, and goatskins with brine and then scraping off the hair, they could make something smooth and thin enough for bookmaking.

Parchment or vellum, as it was called, was first used to make scroll books, since people looked to Egyptian books as a model. But soon people realized that parchment had a great advantage over papyrus. While papyrus cracked and broke off when bent, parchment folded easily. When groups of folded sheets were gathered together, sewn through the fold, and bound between strong wooden boards, a new kind of book appeared on the scene.

It took a while for bookmakers to invent portable books. This medieval book, with soft overlapping covers made of leather, was called a girdle book. The knot at the bottom tucked into the owner's girdle, or belt, and the book swung down when not in use.

A monk in the 1100s in Germany makes a book by

scraping hairs off stretched goatskin

cutting and trimming a sheet

preparing a pen

Early European books were made with great care, and each step was done by hand. First the parchment was treated, stretched, scraped, and trimmed down to size. Then an expert writer called a **scribe** used a sharp piece of bone and a ruler to draw barely visible lines on each sheet. (The blue lines on your notebook paper, called **rules,** are just a modern version of the lines people drew in the Middle Ages.)

After ruling, the scribe sharpened a quill pen and began copying down the text, letter by letter, word by word. The scribe left room for decorations and drawings to be done by an artist called an **illuminator**. All of these steps could take months, even years, and the book still had to be bound!

erasing a mistake

sewing together groups of pages

and preparing the wooden cover.

其二

This wood-block illustration from Japan shows a papermaker at work. All of the picture that you can see stands up in relief from a carved block of wood. When the areas in relief are covered with ink, they print as black lines. Wherever you see white, the wood on the block has been carved away.

While European scribes were slowly copying word after word onto parchment, Asian bookmakers had managed to invent both paper and printing. They made their paper by boiling plants and then straining the softened fibers through a mold. When the sheets of paper dried, they were strong and flexible and easy to fold.

To print on their paper, Asian bookmakers took blocks of wood and carved away portions of the top layer. They kept carving until a design—often of words and pictures—was left. The design stood out in relief from the rest of the woodblock, and people still speak today of **relief printing**.

Relief printing then and now is very simple. Once you have a design cut in relief, spread ink on it and press it into paper. (If you've ever decorated paper with potato prints, you've done relief printing.)

The inked design is transferred onto the paper, but not exactly as it was in the original design. The printed result will always be the mirror image of the original. Asian wood-block cutters had to cut designs backward in order for the printed version of their woodblock to read right.

When Johann Gutenberg first began experimenting with printing books in Europe in the 1400s, he too used relief printing. For each of the twenty-six letters of the alphabet, and for some combinations of letters, he created small pieces of metal **type**. One end of the type was flat, and on the other end was the design of a letter, backward and in relief. By arranging many pieces of type in the flat bed of a printing press—something Gutenberg also invented—he could print two pages of text at a time. The Bible that Gutenberg printed in about 1456 is one of the most beautiful books ever made.

Above: *Gutenberg's Bible is the first book printed with movable type.* Right: *Type*

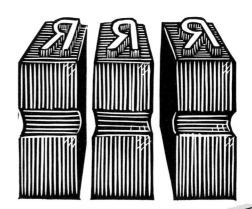

Nowadays nearly all books are printed and bound mechanically. Nearly all are made of machine-made paper. And sometimes it seems as if nearly all books look alike and look boring. But they don't have to.

People around the world make unique and unusual books by hand. Sometimes the books they make don't look at all like books on the shelves of your library or local bookstore.

Does a book have to be square or rectangular? Barbara Harmon, the author of *Some Mountains,* decided that her book would be shaped like a mountain. Although her text is only ten words long, both the words and the shape of the book work together to tell a many-layered story.

Once you start making books of your own by hand, you may never look at a book in the same way again. What kind of book will you make? Read on and decide.

Artist Barbara Harmon decided to make a book whose shape reflects her story: "Some mountains are so high they create their own weather."

II. Getting Started

Finding Your Story

So you want to make a book. First, you need to find your story. But where do story ideas come from?

People who write for a living say that ideas for stories are all around us. To find your story, you'll need to train your eyes and ears and nose. Writing takes some practice, so grab a pencil and paper or a computer and start putting down your thoughts.

Look at the world around you. What's the story behind the kid sitting next to you, the one who hasn't said a word to you all semester? Can you imagine why he's so quiet? Can you write a description that will help readers "see" him, just through the words you've put on the page?

Or look out the window. When you see the first robin of spring singing in a tree, can you imagine the story of how it spent its winter vacation? Is it worn out with all that flying or is it eager to build its new nest?

Story Starters

Here are a few surefire questions to help you start a story:
- What was the best trip you ever took?
- What kinds of funny or silly things does your pet do?
- What musical instrument do you play and what do you like, or dislike, about it?
- What was your greatest moment, so far, in sports history?

Stories can open up a window on the outside world, but they can also give you a way of seeing your own future. What would your story be if you were a race-car driver trying to grab the lead in the very last lap? Would your palms be sweaty? Would you be able to hear anything over the roar of the engines?

Would you cough at the smell of gasoline and burning tire rubber and engine fumes? All of these details can help make your story real to your readers.

If you prefer facts to made-up stories, then act like a reporter. You can track down stories—and histories—in your own home. What do your grandparents remember of the Civil Rights movement? Can your parents remember how it felt to watch the first people walk on the moon? Ask just a few questions of the folks around you, and you'll probably have more stories than you know what to do with.

You might think you need a written-out story, but you don't have to be a writer to make a book. A picture can paint a thousand, or at least a couple dozen, words. Several pictures or other images linked together in the pages of a book can tell a whole story, with or without words.

Right: *Artist Sandra Boynton tells stories with words and pictures.*

Visual books rely on pictures to tell a story. Other books use words instead. Many books combine both words and pictures. When you have a story—in words or in pictures or both—it's important to plan ahead.

Planning Ahead

Publishers call the planning stage "design and layout." If you are working with a text, write it out and decide where you want to divide it into pages. A change in scene, for example, may be a good place for a page break. You may also want to begin a new page when a new character begins speaking.

If you are making a visual book, think about the pictures you want to draw. Sketch out your ideas and arrange the images in the order that will best tell your story.

Once you've divided the text into pages or put your pictures in order, take a large sheet of paper, mark it off into boxes about the size of a page in a book, and place the text or images in the boxes.

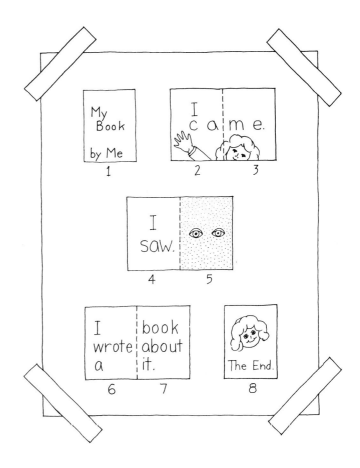

This layout is for a book with eight pages. When you open the finished book, you'll see pages 2–3, 4–5, and 6–7 side by side with a fold in between.

If you're making a book with text but you want to illustrate different pages, sketch out your ideas on the layout.

For some of the bindings you'll find later in this book, you will want to arrange your text and pictures in special ways to take advantage of how the pages turn or fold or unroll (in the case of a scroll). For books like these, you should make a **dummy,** or a trial-run book. A dummy may sound silly, but it's really very smart.

Make your dummy book the same size and shape as the book you want to create. It should have the same number of pages as you plan to have in your finished book. It should have all the words and sketches of all the pictures, just where you want them to be. And, if you're like most bookmakers, your dummy will have lots of crossed-out words or redrawn sketches or new things pasted in on top of old things. A dummy is a place to try out ideas, to make mistakes and changes, and to work to create the best finished book possible.

When your layout or your dummy is finished, you can begin choosing the materials for your book.

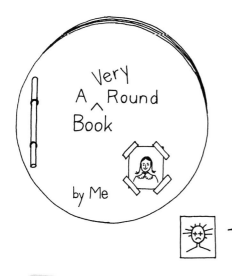

A dummy is the same size and shape as the finished book. It even has the same kind of binding, so you will know for sure that you can bind your book in this way.

← The picture of me I decided not to use after I tried it in the dummy

Materials

To make books by hand, you'll need a few basic materials. They are a paper punch, scissors, glue, and paper. Here are a few specialized tools that you may want to put on your materials list:

●An awl is used to punch small holes through pieces of paper. It makes it easier for bookbinders to push and pull through a needle and thread when they are making a traditional sewn binding. For the projects shown in this book, you can use a paper punch or a pushpin instead of an awl. If you do use an awl, be careful not to poke yourself with the sharp pointed end.

●A bone folder is a piece of bone that makes it easier to fold paper. It can come in handy when your hands and fingers aren't clean and you need to make a sharp, clean fold. If you don't have a bone folder, just use your thumbnail pressed against the paper—and remember to clean your thumb first!

●PVA, or polyvinyl acetate, is a strong, quick-drying glue available at most art supply stores. Elmer's and glue sticks aren't as strong as PVA, but they can be used for most of the projects in this book.

●Most of the projects in this book require a pair of scissors. But for some cutting, you may also want to use an X-acto knife. BE CAREFUL. The X-acto knife's blade is razor sharp. Always cover the knife edge when not in use. If you are at all uncertain about using an X-acto knife, ask an adult to make the cuts for you. This kind of knife can cut deeply, so be sure to put a layer of stiff board between the paper you want to cut and the table or other surface underneath.

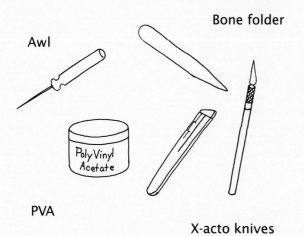

Awl

Bone folder

PVA

PolyVinyl Acetate

X-acto knives

III. Paper

Handmade Paper

The most important material in any book is paper. While most of the paper you see is machine made, people have been making paper by hand for centuries. To make paper by hand, you will need:

2 flat wooden frames, the same size

nylon mesh or netting, 50 mesh per inch

stapler

scrap paper (Do not use glossy paper.)

blender

dishpan

1 or 2 boards, larger than the frames

old newspapers

synthetic, disposable kitchen cloths or papermaking felts

mesh strainer (optional)

cookie cutters (optional)

cup (optional)

turkey baster (optional)

iron

spray starch

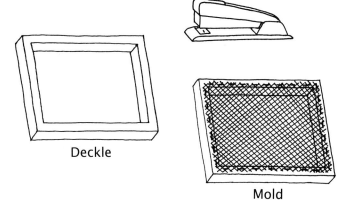

Deckle

Mold

1   Take two wooden frames and remove the glass and backing. Measure enough mesh to fit across one frame. Staple it snugly to all four sides of the frame, making sure the netting is taut. This will be your mold. The other half of the frame is called a deckle. The deckle works with the mold to shape each sheet of paper. They fit together one on top of the other, with the deckle on top, the mold on the bottom, and the mesh in between—like a mesh sandwich. Set this aside.

Blender two-thirds full of water and paper to be pulped

Dishpan two-thirds full of water and pulp

2 Take a stack of scrap paper and tear each sheet into bits no more than an inch across—about the size of postage stamps. Drop them into the blender until it is half full. Add water until the blender is two-thirds full. Ask an adult to blend the paper bits in short, five-second bursts on low about fifteen times.

3 When the paper is cut up so much that you see only small bits, like lumps in oatmeal, transfer this pulp into the dishpan. Continue blending paper and water and emptying the pulp into the dishpan until the pan is about half full. Add water until the dishpan is two-thirds full.

4 If you want colored pulp—and colored paper—start with colored paper bits in the blender. Save sheets of scrap paper in a particular color to blend together for a batch of pulp. Try decorating your pulp. Small flowers, glitter, and other small, flat objects can also be added to the pulp once it's in the dishpan.

About Deckles and Molds . . .
Here are a few options for inexpensive deckles and molds:
● Canvas stretchers, sold at art supply stores, are less expensive than picture frames and can be put together to make a deckle and mold.
● Use an embroidery hoop as your mold, stretching the netting across it, just as you would stretch fabric to embroider on. You don't need a deckle, just hold the hoop level and let the excess pulp drain off the sides. Your mold will make round sheets, so start thinking about stories that will fit into a round book!

5 After you've prepared the pulp, you'll need to make a **mound**. This is where you will put the new sheets of paper. Take a board (or a cookie sheet or another flat surface) and place it where water can drain from it safely. Fold a few sheets of old newspaper into shapes about the size of your deckle and mold. Put the folded sheets on the board and cover them with a dishcloth or felt. Pour a cupful of water over the mound to soak.

About the Pulp . . .

As you make more and more sheets of paper, the mix in the dishpan will have more water and less pulp. Your first sheets of paper will be quite thick, but later sheets will be thinner and thinner. If you want sheets of equal thickness, use a mesh strainer to remove some of the pulp from the dishpan. Set it aside in a cup. As the sheets of paper become thinner, add the pulp back in.

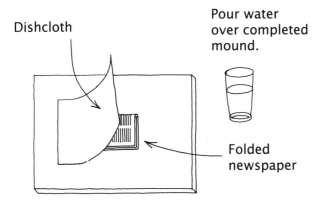

Dishcloth

Pour water over completed mound.

Folded newspaper

6 From this step on, you will probably want to wear an apron or raincoat and maybe even rubber boots. Papermaking is messy. First you must "wake up" the pulp. That means running your fingers through the pulp in the dishpan to mix it well with the water. ▶

7 Next take your mold and deckle in both hands and hold it out in front of you as if you were going to hang it up like a picture. The deckle should be facing you. Beginning at the far end of the dishpan, bring the deckle and mold through the pulp in one motion. Drag your knuckles along the bottom of the pan as you go. When you pull the deckle and mold up from the water, hold it level over the dishpan and let water drain through the mesh.

Separating the deckle and mold

8 Once most of the water has drained, set the deckle and mold on the edge of the dishpan and carefully remove the deckle. Set it aside. Hold the mold in both hands and in one motion turn it all the way over, laying it flat on the damp cloth and newspapers. Papermakers call this step **couching** (pronounced COOCH-ing). They lay the sheet down to rest on the cloth, just as you might lie down on a couch for a nap. Press gently against the mold and then pull up. The new sheet of paper should stick to the cloth.

Couching one sheet on top of the other

9 While the paper is still wet, you can "draw" pictures on it with paper pulp. Take a cupful of pulp made from scrap paper of a different color. Position a cookie cutter on top of the paper. Pour the colored pulp inside the cookie cutter or use a turkey baster to squirt pulp evenly inside the cookie-cutter shape. Let it sit for a few minutes before you remove the cookie cutter.

10 You can keep on decorating your sheet as long as it's still damp. If you have different-sized molds, couch a second, smaller sheet in a different color on top of the first. Or cut words out of the newspaper and gently press them onto your newly formed sheet. The words should stick without any glue. ▼

About Pulp Painting . . .

With a turkey baster and batches of pulp in different colors, you can become a pulp painter. Place your deckle and mold over the dishpan so water can drain through.

Then use the turkey baster to cover the mold with pulp. Squiggly lines, blobs, and squirts of pulp just come naturally once you've loaded your turkey baster.

11 Once you've finished decorating, place a second cloth on top of the wet sheet of paper. Continue to stack new sheets between cloths. When you make your last sheet, cover it with another cloth. To begin drying the paper, use a rolling pin to press out as much of the water as possible. Or put a second board on top of the stack, take the stack outdoors, and stand on top of it. Papermakers use hand or mechanical presses instead of rolling pins or feet. They call this step "weeping." When you see how much water is pressed out of the paper, you'll know how it got that name.

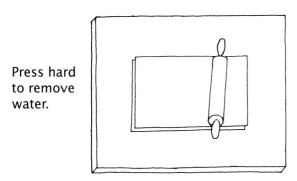

Press hard to remove water.

12 Once you have squeezed out as much water as you can, begin peeling apart the cloths. The paper should cling to the cloths. Spread old newspapers on a flat, dry surface (a tile floor works well) and lay the cloths and paper out to dry. Let the sheets dry overnight. The next day, have an adult help you by ironing each cloth and paper at a medium setting.

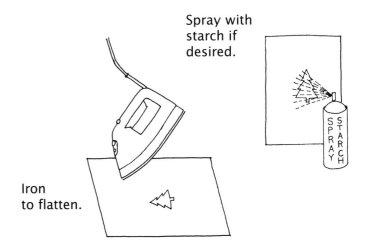

Spray with starch if desired.

Iron to flatten.

Once the paper is dry, you can pull it up from the cloth and spray it with starch. (The starch helps keep ink from running when you write on the paper. In the Middle Ages, scribes used a mixture made from egg whites for the same purpose.)

13 Never pour extra paper pulp down the drain. It will cause clogging. Use a strainer to remove the water and then throw out the pulpy part. Or place extra pulp in sealed plastic bags and store in the freezer for future papermaking.

Marbled Paper

Traditionally, bookmakers have used decorated papers for the endsheets of books. Often these papers have been **marbled,** or dipped in a paint bath. In Ebru marbling, combs are used to move paints on top of water thickened with something called carrageenan. *Ebru* means "cloud art" in Turkish, and this kind of marbling was invented in Turkey in the 1400s.

For Ebru marbling, you should begin preparing materials at least one day in advance. Put on some old clothes or an apron before you begin. The colors used in marbling seem to get on everything, and they can be difficult to wash out. You will need:

powdered carrageenan (available from art supply stores or the resources listed on page 63)
blender
bucket
shallow tub
pencil
paper, cut smaller than the tub
white vinegar
spray bottle
sponge
board, larger than the sheets of paper
acrylic paints
cups or jars
old newspapers
eyedroppers
sticks, skewers, toothpicks, old combs

1　Following package instructions, mix carrageenan with water in a blender. While instructions may vary, to make 1½ gallons of mix, you should fill your blender with 6 cups of water, add 1 tablespoon of carrageenan, and blend for 30 seconds.

Empty the liquid into a bucket. Repeat this step twice, then fill the blender once more with water to rinse. Add that water to the bucket. Let it sit for about 24 hours, or as directed by the supplier. Stir every 8 hours or so. Be sure the mixture is well blended (no white lumps) and at room temperature. At the correct consistency, carrageenan is very slimy. It's okay to touch it to test it. It shouldn't smell bad; if it does, it has spoiled. The mix should keep for 2 or 3 days. Pour enough of the mixture into the shallow tub so that it's at least 1 inch deep.

2 Prepare the paper by marking each sheet with an X. Pour vinegar into the spray bottle. Spray each sheet with vinegar on the side without an X. (Vinegar helps the colors stick to the paper. The X will tell you which side isn't coated.) Use a clean sponge to spread the vinegar spray evenly. Stack the sheets vinegar side down under a board. While the paper is going from wet to just damp, mix your paints. Put small amounts of paint into cups or jars and mix to desired colors. Then add water until the paint is as thick as cream.

Too Slimy?

So you'd like to try marbling, but you aren't ready to dip into slimy carrageenan? Then you might want to try Japanese paper marbling instead of Ebru marbling. Boku-Undo Co., Ltd., makes a Japanese marbling set with no slime and very little mess. Apart from the kit, all you need is paper, water, and a shallow tub. The kit, with full instructions, is sold in art supply stores and through the suppliers listed at the end of this book.

Spray with vinegar,
then spread with sponge.

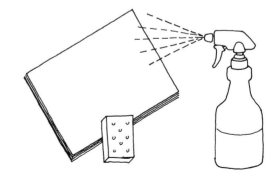

3 Take a waste sheet of paper and lightly drag it over the surface of the mixture in the tub. This will create an even surface tension on which you can drop your paints. Use the eyedroppers to drop paint on the surface. ▼

Each drop of paint will spread into a circle a few inches in diameter. When you've added as much color as you want, grab a stick, toothpick, or comb. Push, pull, or rake it over the paint-covered surface to move colors around.

4 When the pattern is complete, take a sheet of still-damp paper from the pile. Make sure the X faces you. Holding top and bottom corners, lay the paper vinegar side down onto the mixture. Put the paper down using a rolling motion. When all the paper is touching the surface of the mixture, pull it up. ▼

Professional marblers learn to move the colors into many different patterns. They may even become well-known for a pattern they create. Try moving the colors in your tub to form your own one-of-a-kind marbling pattern. ⬥

5 Lay the sheet flat in or near a sink and pour a cup or two of water over it to remove the excess carrageenan. Lay newly marbled sheets paint side up on old newspapers to dry.

6 Before beginning your next sheet, drag a sheet of wastepaper across the top of the mixture to remove the leftover paint.

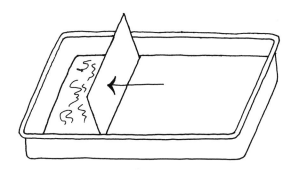

7 When you have finished marbling, pour the dirty carrageenan mix down the toilet. Flush immediately. Clean everything well with warm, soapy water. Acrylic paints are easy to remove when still wet, but can be impossible to remove when dry.

Once you get the hang of marbling paper and making it by hand, you'll need to figure out how to use your new creations. In the next chapter, you'll find many tips on how to use handmade and marbled papers in books.

However you choose to use your papers, it's a good idea to plan ahead. Do you want your book to have marbled-paper covers? Then consider marbling onto construction paper or other paper that is stiff enough for a book cover. If you want a tough but flexible paper cover, then try to make extra-thick sheets of handmade paper.

Handmade sheets of all thicknesses can be used for the pages of the books shown in the next chapter. If you plan to write on your pages, try to choose sheets with a smooth surface. Even after ironing, some handmade sheets are too uneven for easy writing. If that's the case, try adding words and pictures to your handmade-paper pages using the collage techniques described in the last chapter of this book.

IV. Binding

Whether you use paper you make or paper you buy, your next step is to learn about binding. Modern bookbinderies are filled with complex machines. Fortunately, you won't need to use any of them. Binding books by hand is really very simple.

Roll It Up Scroll Book

Probably the simplest kind of book you can make from paper is a scroll. A scroll is a piece of paper rolled up. Adding machine tape is good material for a small scroll. Rolls of shelf paper can be used to make larger scrolls. For a quick scroll book, you will need:

1 sheet 12- by 18-inch construction or handmade
  paper, cut in half lengthwise
glue
scissors
paper punch
ribbon
wastepaper

1 Take one strip of paper and roll it up. You've got a scroll book! Your book can be read two ways:

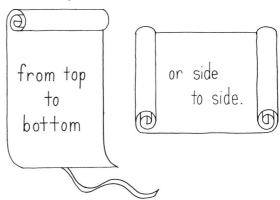

from top to bottom

or side to side.

2 Whichever way you read it, you'll need some way to keep your book from unrolling when it's not in use. One solution is to find or make a container. An empty toilet paper roll makes a handy scroll holder. Just roll your book up tight and slide it in. Use marbled paper to decorate your scroll holder.

3 Ribbon and string will also keep your scroll in a roll. You can tie the ribbon around your scroll book. Or you can make the tie a permanent part of the book. At the beginning or end of your scroll, make a fold, turning in about 1½ inch of the book. (You'll glue this fold shut later, so don't make your fold where you've written or drawn anything you want to save.)

4. Take a scissors and cut off the corners at an angle, cutting through both thicknesses. Then take a paper punch and make a hole in the middle of the folded edge. Be sure your paper punch is right on the fold, not inside the fold.

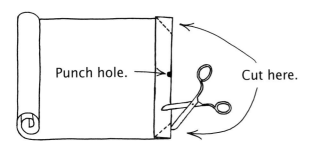

Punch hole. Cut here.

5 Now measure a length of ribbon that's at least 1 foot long. Set it aside. Open the folded end of the book and place it over a waste sheet of paper. Spread glue along the end just to the fold. Slip one end of the ribbon through the hole from the front. Pull about 1 inch of ribbon through the hole. Press that short end down and fold the glued paper over it.

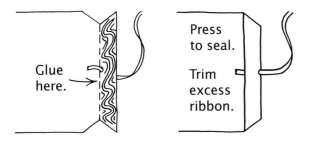

Glue here.

Press to seal.

Trim excess ribbon.

Press hard to seal and trim off any excess ribbon inside the book. Roll up your scroll, wind the ribbon around the book, and slip the end under to secure. ▾

6 To increase the length of your scroll, take another piece of paper the same width and put it on a waste sheet of paper. Spread glue on one end, covering about ½ to 1 inch. Lay that glued end over the unfolded end of the scroll book and press hard to seal.

Small, Tall Sewn Book

Europeans in the Middle Ages bound their books by sewing through parchment from the inner fold to the outer edge, or **spine.** The book below isn't made from calf- or goatskin, but you'll sew it in much the same way as medieval bookbinders did. For this book, you will need:

1 sheet 8½- by 11-inch paper
scissors
1 sheet construction or thick, handmade paper
paper clips
awl or pushpin
thread or embroidery floss
needle

1 Cut the sheet of paper in half lengthwise. Then cut each piece in half, making four sheets of paper, about 5½ by 4¼ inches. Stack your sheets and choose a stiffer paper (construction and handmade papers work well) for the cover. When measuring the cover, make it just as tall as the sheets and about ¼ inch wider.

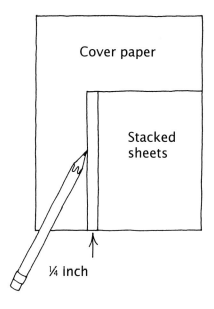

Cover paper

Stacked sheets

¼ inch

2 Now take your sheets of paper and fold each one in half lengthwise to make four long and tall **folios,** or folded sheets. Nest them one inside the other. Then fold the cover paper in half and wrap it around the inside pages. If the inside pages are sticking out beyond the cover, this is a good time to trim the pages or to measure and cut a new cover.

3 Find the innermost fold and open the book flat. Put a paper clip at the top and bottom of each half of the book. This will keep the pages and cover from shifting when you bind the book.

Clip pages and cover together.

5 Measure a length of thread or embroidery floss about three times the height of the book. Thread your needle. To sew, hold the needle in one hand and the half-open book in the other. Sew in the direction pictured.

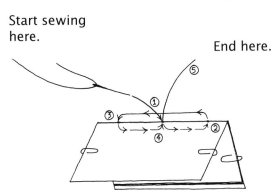

Start sewing here.

End here.

4 Ask an adult to make sewing holes with an awl or a pushpin. Holding the book half-open, the adult should poke small holes from the inner fold through to the cover in three places: about ⅝ inch from the head, or top of the book; in the middle; and about ⅝ inch from the tail, or bottom of the book.

6 Pull gently on the loose ends of thread to tighten. Make sure each end lies on either side of the long stitch down the spine. Tie the loose ends in a double or square knot around the long thread. Trim the ends down to about ½ inch. Remove paper clips.

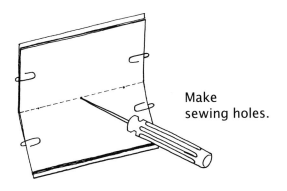

Make sewing holes.

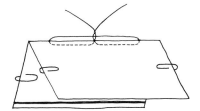

Pull ends gently to tighten, then tie.

Bind It Up the Side Books

In Japan and China, bookbinders piled sheets of paper on top of each other and stitched along the outside of the spine. Asian bookbinders left this side-sewing visible, using complex and beautiful sewing patterns to decorate their books.

The books that follow are all based on traditional Asian book forms, although they don't require a needle and thread.

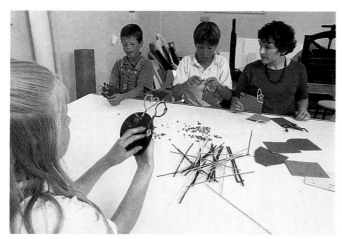

In Bind It Up the Side Books, the binding is part of the decoration.

Your books can be any size, but for the instructions below, you will need:

2 to 3 sheets 8½- by 11-inch paper
scissors
1 sheet construction or thick, handmade paper
paper clips
paper punch
stick and rubber band or pipe cleaners

1 Cut each sheet of 8½- by 11-inch paper in half once and then in half again for sheets about 4¼ by 5½ inches. To make covers, cut two sheets, the same size as your text sheets, from a stiffer paper. Stack the text pages between the two covers and paper clip along the long sides. (These sides will be the head and tail of your book.)

2 With a paper punch, make two holes about 1 inch from the side and 1 inch from the head and tail.

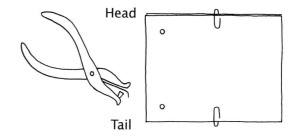

3 To bind the book, try one of the options shown on this page:

Pipe Cleaners

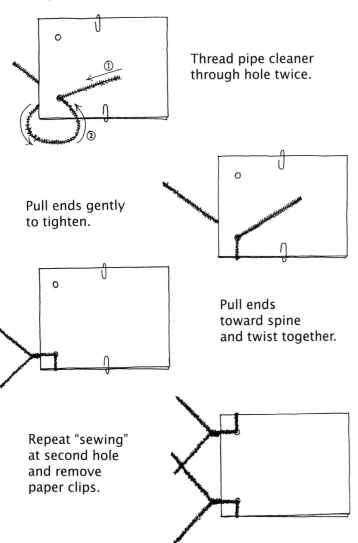

Thread pipe cleaner through hole twice.

Pull ends gently to tighten.

Pull ends toward spine and twist together.

Repeat "sewing" at second hole and remove paper clips.

Stick and Rubber Band

Slip rubber band around stick and pass loose end through binding hole.

Pulling the loose end of the rubber band through the second hole, slip it over the free end of the stick.

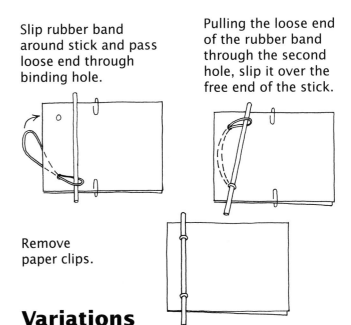

Remove paper clips.

Variations

Take a look at the section on windows on page 48 to make your book unique. Or combine the pipe cleaner binding with pages cut into the shape of a snake or a strange creature.

Fold It Up Books

This kind of book has a lot of nick-names: accordion, window blind, zig-zag. All of these names should tell you something about how the book is made. You can use any size or length paper, but for these instructions, you will need:

1 sheet 12- by 18-inch lightweight construction or handmade paper

scissors

1 small strip of paper (optional)

glue (optional)

1 Cut the sheet of paper into two long equal strips. Take one strip and fold it in half, bringing the short ends together. Fold short ends back to the first fold to make a W-shape. Take short ends again and fold to the nearest fold (the second and third folds). You'll end up with a triple V-shape. Take the small V-shapes and fold point A to fold B and then point C to fold B. Fold the sections back on themselves. You now have an accordion fold in 8 equal sections. Folded up, the book should measure about 2¼ by 6 inches.

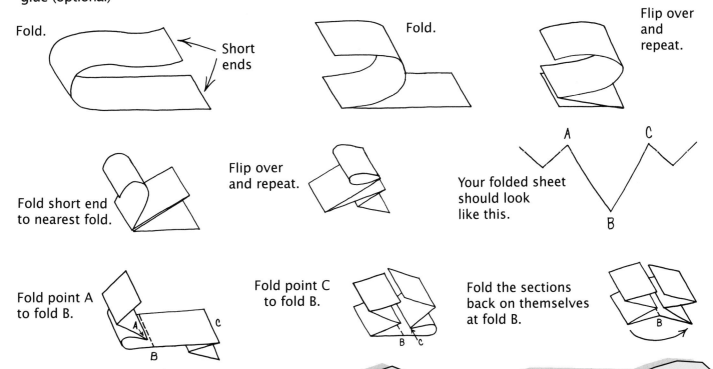

Fold.

Short ends

Fold.

Flip over and repeat.

Fold short end to nearest fold.

Flip over and repeat.

Your folded sheet should look like this.

A   C

B

Fold point A to fold B.

Fold point C to fold B.

Fold the sections back on themselves at fold B.

Fold It Up Books

2 If you've folded the paper as shown above, you'll have 8 equal sections or 16 pages, using both sides. To lengthen a Fold It Up Book, make another 8-section accordion as directed above. Then cut a strip of paper the same height as your book and about 1 inch wide. Fold the strip in half lengthwise. Place the V-shaped strip on a piece of wastepaper. Cover the strip with glue and attach the strip first to one accordion and then to the other. Take care that the cut ends of the accordions meet at the fold in the strip.

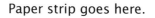

Paper strip goes here.

3 You can use this glued strip method to join together long accordions and shorter sections. Let's say each person in your class or group makes a folded sheet, or folio, on the same theme. You can join the folios together to make a long accordion, using the glued strip method. Fold It Up Books can be lengthened in more than one way. Let your imagination take you in different directions:

Sew in a Small, Tall Sewn Book
or another Fold It Up Book at a fold.

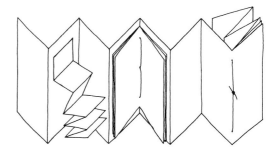

Glue in
a smaller
Fold It Up Book.

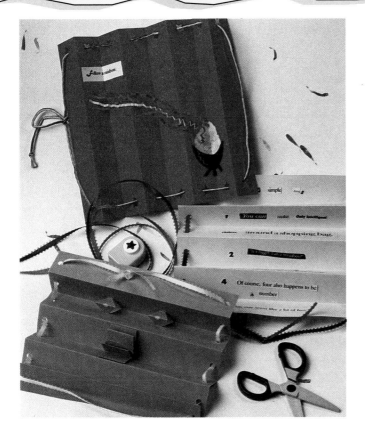

1. Take the sheet of paper and fold it as shown on page 41. Once your book is folded, use a paper punch to make holes at either end, ½ inch from the edges. Punch through each page separately.

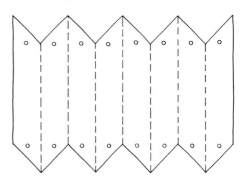

Punch holes near the edges.

Window Blind Variation
This Fold It Up Book will look right at home, either shading your window or hanging around your neck. You will need:

1 sheet of 9- by 12-inch lightweight construction or handmade paper

paper punch

string or yarn

2. To bind, take enough string to run through the holes and wrap around the book with room to spare. With the book folded up, guide the string through the holes and tie the ends together in a knot. This book can be decorated, drawn on, written on, and then slipped over the maker's head—to be worn as a book necklace!

Thread string through holes and tie ends.

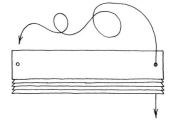

Flag Book Variation

In this book, an accordion fold is built right into the spine. You can use any size paper, but for the instructions below, you will need:

5 sheets 9- by 12-inch construction or handmade paper in different colors

glue

scissors

1 Fold one sheet of construction paper into a 9-inch-long accordion as shown on page 41. This will be the spine. Fold two sheets in half bringing the short ends together. These folded sheets will be the front and back covers. Take the spine piece and draw a thin line of glue along one end. Open up one of the covers. Line up one end against the glued spine.

Press down. Then draw another line of glue on the spine, on the side opposite your first line of glue. Fold the cover over the spine piece and press down. Do the same for the other cover, attaching it to the opposite end of the spine piece.

2 Now take the remaining sheets and cut them in half, to make sheets that are 9 by 6 inches. Take each of these sheets and cut them into thirds, 3 by 6 inches. These will be the pages of the book.

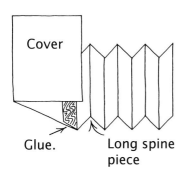

Cover

Glue.　　Long spine piece

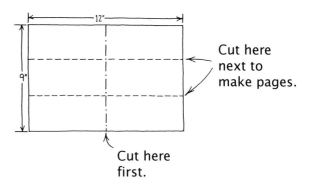

Cut here next to make pages.

Cut here first.

3 Lay your book flat so you can see three "hills," or high folds between the covers. Choose three pages from your pile of colored strips. Start at the head of the book and position the strips along the "hills" as shown. ▼ ▶

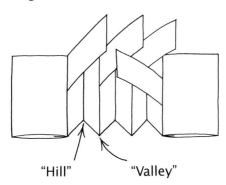

"Hill"   "Valley"

4 Now draw a thin line of glue along the edge of each strip and press it against the spine. Do the same for the other "hill" folds, alternating the direction of the pages as you move down the spine. You will have a few left-over pages. Save these for your next Flag Book.

5 Allow your book to dry. Then try reading through the pages. This book can be read by turning each group of three pages just as you would turn a page in a normal book. But if you take a cover in each hand and pull gently in opposite directions, you're in for a surprise—your book can also be read as one big page.

Pop-Ups and Windows

Do you want to add something extra to your books? Try opening a window or making things pop up. These pop-ups can be worked into all of the bindings described in this chapter except for the Bind It Up the Side Book. For fun additions to that kind of binding, see the section on windows.

Basic Pop-Up

For a basic pop-up, you will need:

1 unbound folio, or folded sheet
pencil
scissors

1 Take a folio and draw two short lines from the fold toward the opposite edge. The top line should point down, and the bottom line should point up. The lines shouldn't meet.

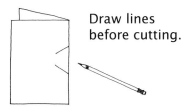

Draw lines before cutting.

2 Cut along your lines, starting from the fold and going through both thicknesses. Be careful not to cut too far. Open the folio and press the cut part from the outside of the folio to the inside until it pops up. Then close the folio to recrease the folds in your pop-up.

What is it? Maybe it's the beak of an owl or the third eye of a monster. You decide. Try these variations or make up your own:

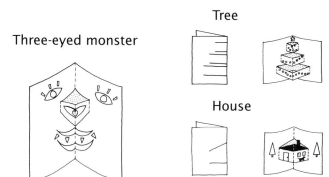

Three-eyed monster

Tree

House

Accordion Pop-Up

For this pop-up, you will need:

1 unbound folio, or folded sheet
long strip of paper
glue
scissors (optional)

1 Using the long strip of paper, make a Fold It Up Book that's smaller than your folio. (See page 41 for folding instructions.) Glue one end of the smaller book and center it inside the folio. Glue the other end of the accordion and close the folio over it. Open the folio to reveal the folding pop-up within your book.

2 Want to make your pop-up even more unusual? Before gluing, cut the smaller Fold It Up Book into a special shape. You can make a paper chain of people, hearts, pumpkins, or trees to fit inside your book. Be sure that whatever picture you cut extends to the folded edges of the accordion. You don't want to cut through all of the fold.

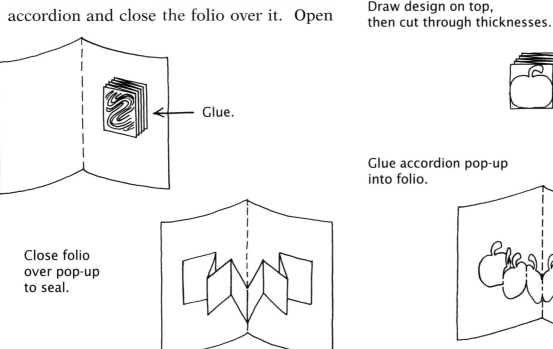

Glue.

Close folio over pop-up to seal.

Draw design on top, then cut through thicknesses.

Glue accordion pop-up into folio.

Windows

Windows work especially well in Bind It Up the Side Books on pages 39 and 40, but they do require some planning. Be sure to make and insert windows before you bind your book.

For one window, you will need:

1 piece of paper, cut according to instructions below
pencil
X-acto knife
paper punch
glue (optional)

1 Once you know the page size for your Bind It Up the Side Book, cut one page that's just as high as the others, but twice as long. Fold the sheet in half to make a page that's a double thickness. The folded edge will go along the **fore edge,** the side opposite the spine.

Fold paper in half.

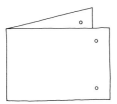

2 Open the folded sheet and use your pencil to trace three sides of a window on the inside of one of the pages. Use an X-acto knife to cut along your lines.

Draw window on inside,

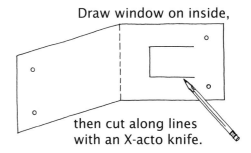

then cut along lines
with an X-acto knife.

3 Refold the sheet, pull open the window, and fold it back. What can you see through this window? That's up to you. Decorate the inside of the other half of your sheet with a surprising scene. Or glue in a picture. Bind the finished window into your book, following the instructions on page 40.

Fold shut. Pull
the window open
and crease.

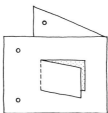

Attach
a picture
behind window.

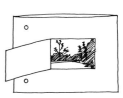

Closures and Covers

Some books aren't meant to be left open for everyone to read. On the next pages, you'll find ways to cover up and close your most secret books.

Tie It Shut

This ribbon closure works well with Bind It Up the Side and Small, Tall Sewn books. For either binding, you will need:

folded sheets and cover for Small, Tall Sewn
   or Bind It Up the Side books
paper punch
scissors
ribbon
glue
paper clips

1 Measure, cut, and fold the pages and covers for your binding as shown on page 37 or 39. Before securing book pages to covers with paper clips, punch holes in the front and back covers. Make your holes midway down the fore edge, the edge opposite the spine. Be sure to punch your holes as far from the edge as possible. (If a hole is too close to the edge, the ribbon might tear through.)

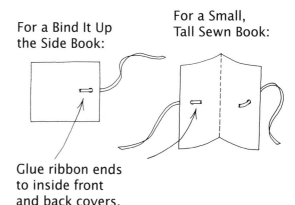

For a Bind It Up the Side Book:

For a Small, Tall Sewn Book:

Glue ribbon ends to inside front and back covers.

2 Cut two pieces of ribbon, each about 8 to 12 inches long. Lead one ribbon through each hole until about 1 inch of ribbon is inside each cover. Apply a small amount of glue to the short ends of ribbon and press them down onto the inside of each cover. Let the glue dry for a few minutes.

3 Next attach the covers to the book pages with paper clips. Bind the book as shown on page 38 or 40. Once the book is bound, remove the paper clips. Use the long ribbon ends to tie the book shut. Either tie a bow or knot at the fore edge or wrap the ribbons around the book once and tie at the spine.

Cover It Up

For this closure, you will need:

folded pages for the Fold It Up Book
thin cardboard
1 9- by 12-inch sheet lightweight construction
 or marbled paper
scissors
glue
ribbon
wastepaper (optional)

1 Make a Fold It Up Book following the instructions on page 41. You will be gluing the top and bottom pages to the covers, so be sure your story doesn't start or end on those pages. Have an adult measure and cut two pieces of thin cardboard about ½ inch taller and wider than your book. These will be your cover boards. Cut two pieces of cover paper (lightweight construction paper and marbled paper work well). The cover paper should be 1 inch taller and wider than the cover boards.

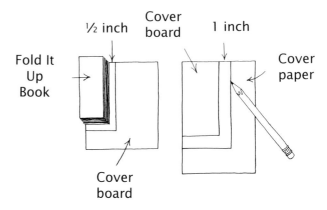

2 Apply glue to the inside of one sheet of cover paper. Center one cover board over it and press it down to glue. With a scissors, cut off the four corners at an angle. Be sure not to cut the paper all the way to the corners of the cover boards. Leave about a board thickness of cover paper sticking out beyond the corners.

Apply glue to cover paper.

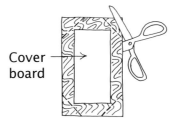

Cut off corners
near the cover board.

3 Now fold the top and bottom, pressing the cover paper close to the board. (You may need to reapply glue.) Pinch the cover paper against the board at each corner with your forefinger and thumb or a bone folder. Fold over the last two sides. Do the same with the second cover. (If you are using regular white glue or a glue stick and the cover paper is not sticking well to the boards, then you may want to switch to a stronger glue, such as PVA.)

Fold top and bottom first, then pinch in corners before folding sides.

4 Decide which will be the front cover and set the back cover aside. Measure a length of ribbon about 2 feet long. Find the center point of the ribbon by folding it in half. Apply glue to about 1 inch of the ribbon at its midpoint. Press the glued ribbon down, centering it inside the front cover.

Glue ribbon to inside front cover. 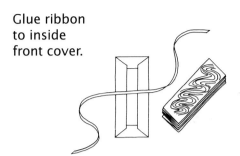 Apply glue to first page of book and attach to front cover.

5 Take your folded-up book, called the book block, and carefully apply glue to the first page. You may want to slip a piece of wastepaper in between that page and the rest of the book when gluing. Next press the book block down, centering it on the inside front cover. Apply glue to the back of the last page, again protecting the rest of the book with a waste sheet of paper. Take the back cover and position it over the book block. Be sure that one cover is centered over the other. Press hard. When the book is dry, wrap the ribbon around the book and tie to close.

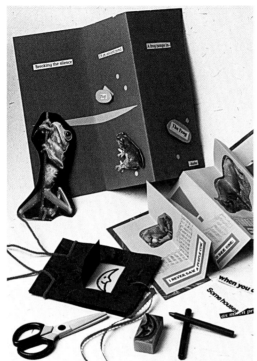

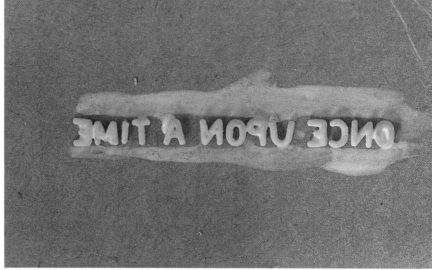

V. Printing and Illustrating

Knowing how to create beautiful, wild, and funny bookbindings from your own handmade paper is only part of the story of making books by hand. To make any book complete, you'll need to find some way to put your story—in words or pictures or both—onto the pages.

Words onto Paper

Writing your own book by hand is probably the simplest and cheapest way of putting words onto paper. If you decide to be your own scribe, you'll be taking part in a long and honored tradition. Even today, hundreds of years after they were made, books from the Middle Ages are known for their beautiful handwritten texts, decorated letters, and colorful hand-painted pictures.

A medieval scribe at work

To put your words onto the page in a beautiful way, follow these tips from medieval scribes. Plan carefully. If your paper is unlined, draw faint guidelines on it so your handwriting doesn't slant up or down. Leave room for decorations or illustrations. And consider decorating the first letter of your story or the first letter in each section. The decorated initials on this page, from the Middle Ages and from today, may give you some ideas.

If handwriting isn't your style, type your text onto paper and glue the paper into your book. Try arranging the text in a way that goes along with the theme of the book. If you are writing a story about an ocean, make the words rise and fall like waves. Draw a decorative frame around the text if you like.

In this illuminated manuscript, a capital letter B almost fills the page.

Press-on lettering is another option. This form of lettering is sold in sheets at art supply stores. Position the sheet so the letter you want lies over the page, just where you want that letter to print. Then take a pencil and rub the back of the sheet until the letter sticks to the page. Press-on lettering looks especially neat if you rule the page first.

If you have a computer handy, you may be able to set your own type and print out your story. Try to choose type that fits the mood of your story. Big bold type styles work well for shocking events.

EGAD!!

For a tall tale, you might want something tall and skinny.

Alice was as tall as a silo.

Decorated and Illustrated Books

Whether you plan to combine words and pictures or make a purely visual book, you can choose from many different ways of decorating and illustrating.

Pasta Blocks

Before Johann Gutenberg invented type, he spent a lot of time hanging around with metal workers. Because of his observations, he made type from metal. But who knows. If he had gone to a grocery store and found alphabet pasta, the history of printing might have been very different. To print from a pasta printing block, you will need:

squares of cardboard
scissors
alphabet and other uncooked pasta
water-based paints
paintbrush
paper
old newspapers

1 Cut out small squares of cardboard, about 2 by 2 inches. Glue pasta onto the cardboard squares to make different designs.

If you use alphabet pasta, remember to glue the letters down backward. (That way, the words will read right when printed.) You'll have the best results if you put each word on a separate block.

2 Pasta comes in all shapes and sizes, but not all kinds are easy to print from. Be sure that each piece of pasta sticks up from the block the same distance. (Skinnier pieces next to thinner ones won't print.)

3 Allow pasta blocks to dry and gather different colors of poster, tempera, or other water-based paints. When the block is dry, use a paintbrush to coat the top of the pasta with thick, undiluted paint. While you let the paint dry for 1 minute, take a sheet of paper and lay it on top of a stack of old newspapers. Press the block into the paper.

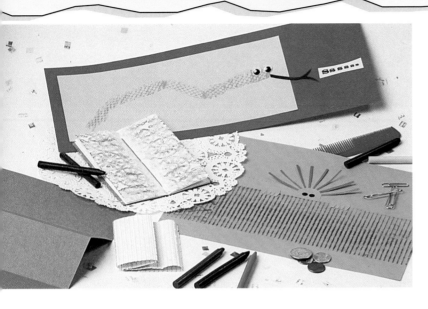

2 Hold the crayon flat against the paper, not point end down, and rub over the object or surface. Rub hard enough so the pattern or design of the object shows, but not so hard that the paper tears. Because there is always some chance of rubbing through the paper, you may want to do your crayon rubbing on a separate sheet of paper and glue it into your book.

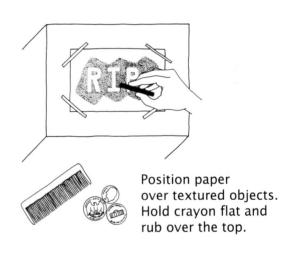

Position paper over textured objects. Hold crayon flat and rub over the top.

Crayon Rubbing
To make a crayon design, you will need:

crayons
flat textured objects or surfaces
fairly thin paper
masking tape (optional)

1 Take the ends of several crayons in different colors and peel off the paper. Gather flat textured objects, such as pennies, combs, or placemats. Or find a flat textured surface such as a heating grate or a gravestone or a manhole cover and position your paper over it. (You may want to secure your paper over the surface with masking tape.)

Eraser Blocks

Relief printing blocks made from gum erasers print evenly and well. Carving a design in the eraser can be tricky and dangerous, so ask an adult to help. To make and print from an eraser block, you will need:

felt-tip marker
gum eraser
X-acto knife
ink pad
paper

1 Take a felt-tip marker and draw the design you want in thick dark lines on one end of a large eraser. Simple designs with strong, bold lines work best. Fill in with marker all the areas that should *not* be cut away.

2 Ask an adult to take an X-acto knife and carve away a layer about ¼ inch deep from the eraser. The adult should remove only

those areas *not* drawn in with marker. When all of the excess eraser is removed, your design will be left, standing in relief. Press your eraser block into a well-inked pad and print it onto paper.

Variation

Potatoes are another good material for relief printing blocks. Cut a potato in half to expose a flat surface. Then use the same methods described above. Bear in mind, however, that potatoes should be fresh and firm, not soft or soggy. Also, remember that potatoes don't last forever. Once you've made your potato printing block, do all the printing you plan to do from that block before it has time to spoil. (Potato printing blocks can be stored in plastic bags in the refrigerator for a few days.)

You can use collage to put just about anything into a book.

No Printing/No Drawing Collage

What if you don't want to write like a scribe, type on a typewriter, draw like an artist, or print like Gutenberg, but you still want to make a book? Don't give up hope, there is plenty of material all around you. Along with a lot of imagination, you will need:

old magazines, newspapers, etc.
scissors
glue
adhesive-backed Velcro (optional)

1 Gather old magazines, newspapers, postcards, junk-mail offers, photos, and other cast-off pieces of printing. Cut out words and images from the magazines and newspapers. Then put the words and images into an order that suggests a story. Glue them into the book form that best helps to tell your story.

2 If you'd rather not glue down your words and images forever, borrow a tool from the astronauts. Space travelers use Velcro to help them hold on to and easily remove objects in their crowded spaceships. You can use it to help your pictures and text move around in your book.

▲ At a fabric or craft store, find a package of small adhesive-backed Velcro buttons. Glue onto stiff paper backing the words and pictures you want to use in your book. Then attach one half of a Velcro button to the backing, another half to the pages of your book. Use one Velcro surface—loops or hooks—on the pages and the other surface on the backs of words and pictures. How does your story change when you move the words and images around?

If you've got the materials, but still aren't sure what kind of story you want to tell, then take a few tips from Dada. Dada is an art movement that started in the early 1900s. The movement's artists tried to find meaning in random combinations of words and images. Their collage pictures were strange and funny and sometimes downright shocking. As a Dada bookmaker, you might grab a bunch of unrelated words and pictures, drop them onto the pages of a book, and glue them in. The story is what you make of it.

That's part of the fun of making books by hand; you make all the choices and decisions. No matter what kind of book you make—a marbled-paper window-blind book or a monster-shaped book covered with rubber-stamp printing—you can be sure that no other book on earth will be quite like yours.

Glossary

codex: a book. This was one of the first words used to describe what we now call a book. It's now used mainly to describe handwritten books.

couching: laying a newly formed sheet of paper to rest and drain on a pile. When a papermaker couches a sheet, the layer of pulp separates from the mold and lies flat.

dummy: a handmade model or mock-up of a book

folios: sheets of paper folded in half. Each folio consists of four pages.

fore edge: the unbound edge of a book opposite the spine

illuminator: a person in medieval times who decorated handwritten books with drawings and designs

marbled: treated with a mixture of paint and carrageenan, or other medium, to create a pattern or design

mound: a dampened pile of newspaper and cloth or papermaking felts onto which newly molded paper is couched and stacked to dry

papyrus: a reedlike plant native to Egypt. Also, the kind of paper made by beating the fibers of the papyrus plant.

parchment: goat-, sheep-, or cowskin that is treated, scraped, and trimmed into thin sheets suitable for bookmaking

quipu: a Peruvian counting or accounts-keeping book made of knotted string

relief printing: the process by which a design or words are cut on a surface in relief, covered with ink, and pressed into paper or cloth

rules: faint lines drawn or scored on paper or parchment to guide scribes and to help them write in straight lines

scribe: a person who writes out documents by hand for a living

scrolls: books that roll up

spine: the part of a book where the pages are bound together

stylus: a metal tool used for writing

tablet: usually a flat slab of clay, stone, or wood. Clay tablets and wooden ones covered with a layer of wax were often used as books in early times.

type: letters, numbers, and symbols used in printing

Bibliography

How Books Are Made

Brookfield, Karen. *Book*. New York: Knopf Books for Young Readers, 1993. A fact- and photo-filled book for all ages.

Burch, Joann Johansen. *Fine Print: A Story about Johann Gutenberg*. Minneapolis: Carolrhoda Books, Inc., 1991. The story of Johann Gutenberg's long, hard struggle to find an alternative to making books by hand.

Edwards, Michelle. *Dora's Book*. Minneapolis: Carolrhoda Books, Inc., 1990. In this picture book, Dora wants to share her memories of Grandma Molly and Grandpa Max with her friends, so she makes a book by hand.

Kehoe, Michael. *A Book Takes Root*. Minneapolis: Carolrhoda Books, Inc., 1993. From a writer's first words scribbled in a notebook, author and photographer Michael Kehoe shows each step in making a picture book.

Laughlin, Sarah, Dana Newman, and Pamela Smith. *Historic Book Arts Projects*. Santa Fe, NM: Press of the Palace of the Governors, 1988. This hand-printed book includes instructions for paper marbling, bookbinding, making a small printing press, and other projects.

Writing and Finding Story Ideas

Bauer, Marion Dane. *What's Your Story?: A Young Person's Guide to Writing Fiction*. New York: Clarion Books, 1992. An award-winning writer shares her tips on how to take ideas and turn them into stories.

Hamley, Dennis. *Hare's Choice*. New York: Doubleday, 1990. In this novel for young readers, a group of children in the same class work together to create a story.

Papermaking and Marbling

Bourgeois, Paulette. *The Amazing Paper Book*. Reading, MA: Addison-Wesley Publishing Company, 1989. Everything you ever wanted to know about paper, plus craft ideas and experiments.

Taylor, Carol. *Marbling Paper & Fabric*. New York: Sterling Publishing Co., Inc., 1991. This book for older readers is full of step-by-step instructions and photos showing the dos and don'ts of marbling.

Watson, David. *Creative Handmade Paper: How to Make Paper from Recycled and Natural Materials*. Turnbridge Wells, England: Search Press, 1991. This excellent photo essay follows in detail all the steps for making handmade paper using inexpensive tools.

Bookbinding and Pop-Ups

Irvine, Joan. *How to Make Pop-Ups*. New York: Morrow Junior Books, 1988. The first of two great books on basic pop-ups, followed by *How to Make Super Pop-Ups* (1992).

Johnson, Paul. *A Book of One's Own: Developing Literacy through Making Books*. Portsmouth, NH: Heinemann, 1992. For both teachers and students, this book covers many different bookbindings and is illustrated by student work.

Smith, Keith. *Non-Adhesive Binding*. Fairport, NY: The Sigma Foundation, 1990. In this classic book for older readers, the author introduces and explains the variety of book forms that can be made without glue.

Handwriting and Low-Tech Printing

Fleischman, Paul. *Copier Creations*. New York: Harper Trophy, 1993. Along with tips on how to use copy machines and where to find clip art, this book includes step-by-step instructions for making flip books.

Jackson, Donald. *The Story of Writing*. London: Taplinger Publishing Company/The Parker Pen Company, 1981. This book for older readers is packed with illustrations of beautiful writing styles.

Resources and Supplies

Several organizations offer classes or exhibitions open to young people interested in the book arts:

Artists Book Works
1422 West Irving Park
Chicago, IL 60613
312/348-4469
Exhibitions showcase artists' books. Workshops for children and adults are offered in papermaking and bookbinding.

Dieu Donné Papermill Inc.
433 Broome Street
New York, NY 10013-2622
212/226-0573
Offers papermaking workshops for children at public schools, museums, and other organizations in New York City.

Minnesota Center for Book Arts
24 North Third Street
Minneapolis, MN 55401
612/338-3634
Displays artists' books and offers classes for children and adults. During the school year, students from area schools come to learn bookbinding, papermaking, and printing firsthand. (Teachers must call to arrange times.)

Specialized papermaking and marbling supplies and books on the book arts are available from the following suppliers:

Colophon Book Arts Supply
3046 Hogum Bay Road, NE
Olympia, WA 98516
206/459-2940

Lee Scott McDonald, Inc.
Fine Hand Papermaking Equipment
P.O. Box 264
Charlestown, MA 02129
617/242-2505

Index

Photo Credits